YOUNG PEOPLE'S STORY OF
OUR HERITAGE

YOUNG PEOPLE'S
STORY OF
OUR HERITAGE

THE AMERICAS
by
V. M. HILLYER and E. G. HUEY

New Edition Designed and Revised by Childrens Press, Chicago

Consultants

William T. Nichol, Principal
Charles Gates Dawes Elementary School, Evanston, Illinois

John R. Lee, Professor of Education
Northwestern University, Evanston, Illinois

Meredith Press, New York

Library of Congress Catalog Card Number: 66-11333

Copyright © 1966 by Meredith Publishing Company. Originally published under the title of *A Child's Geography of the World* by V. M. Hillyer. Revised and Enlarged Edition, with new material by Edward G. Huey. Copyright, 1929, by The Century Co. Copyright, 1951, by Appleton-Century-Crofts, Inc. Copyright, 1957, by Mercantile Safe Deposit and Trust Co. All rights reserved. Printed in the U.S.A. Published simultaneously in Canada.

Contents

Acknowledgments

Cover drawing: The Statue of Liberty, New York
John Hollis-Hollis Associates

Cover photograph: Golden Gate Bridge, San Francisco
Santa Fe Railway Photo

Page 2: Appalachian Mountain region in western Maryland
M. E. Warren, Photography

Frontis: Columbia River Gorge, Oregon
Oregon State Highway Department Photo

Opposite: Children at the zoo in Central Park, New York
New York Convention and Visitors Bureau Photo

———————————

Designed by John Hollis

Edited by Joan Downing

THE AMERICAS

The United States and its Possessions

Introduction

If you were standing on the moon looking at the earth, you would see a great, bright ball reflecting the light of the sun. You might see shadows of the continents.

Earth is a wonderful planet. It is spinning on its axis with the speed of a jet plane. At the same time it is traveling in its orbit around the sun with the speed of a rocket.

Come, make a landing on the earth. As you come near to it you will see that three-quarters of it is water. Head for one of the continents. If you land on a mountain you may not know whether you are in the Alps, or Andes, or Rockies, or even the Himalayas. Mountains are alike in many ways.

If you land in a great city, it might be Tokyo, Cairo, New York, or Rome. Cities are much alike, too.

Photo Courtesy Hong Kong Tourist Association

A harbor full of boats might be Honolulu or Sydney. A wheat field might be in Argentina or Nebraska. There are many things that are alike upon the earth. But there are many things that are different, too. And this is what makes it so interesting.

The earth has been constantly changing over its millions of years. Cracks in its rocky crust have shifted and pushed up as mountain ranges. Heat from within the earth has boiled over in volcanoes that shape the land. Rivers have cut wide V-shaped valleys on the land. Sometimes they have cut deep canyons through solid rock. Glaciers have ground out broad U-shaped valleys and brought fertile soil to places where it had never been before.

Sabena Belgian World Airlines

High mountains along a seacoast may have caused clouds from over the sea to rise and drop their rain along the shore. The far side of the mountains became deserts.

If you put a belt around the broadest part of the globe of the earth you could call it the equator. The earth is tipped on its axis so that this part of it gets the most direct rays of the sun. This is the hottest part of the earth. Jungles flourish here. The North and South Poles of the earth get only slanting rays of the sun. They are ice-bound all year. The earth is a wonder in its own way.

Courtesy of Pan American Union

British Overseas Airways Corporation

Pan American Airways

Yugoslav Consulate, Chicago

American President Lines

British Overseas Airways Corporation

Embassy of Chile, Washington, D.C.

12

You live on this earth. Plants grow on it. Animals make their home on it, from the darkest jungles to the polar ice caps. This is what you will read about in these books. The earth and life upon it.

No matter where you live—on a treeless plain, on a jungle river, in a fertile valley, on a mountainside, on the edge of the desert, on a farm, or in a city—one thing is true. The land you live on affects the way you live. The very first people who came to the land adapted their way of living to what they found. They handed down customs and traditions. This is part of your heritage.

These books will introduce you to people and places you never knew existed.

Even with many words and many, many pictures these books cannot tell you everything. But read them with imagination and with pleasure. You will find you are much more at home on this planet earth, no matter where you live on it.

British Overseas Airways Corporation

Our World from a Distance

Very few of us have ever seen our own world—the planet Earth—all at one time.

You can see a little bit of the world around you—and if you go up into a high building you can see more—and if you go up to the top of a high mountain you can see still more—and if you go up in an airplane you can even see more.

But to see the whole world you would have to go much higher than that. You would have to go into space.

Since most of us have never been in space and have never seen the whole world at one time, how do we know what the world looks like?

A fish in the sea might tell her little fish, "The world is all water—just a huge tub; I've been everywhere and I know."

A camel in the desert might tell her little camels, "The world is all sand—just a huge sand pile; I've been everywhere and I know."

A polar bear on an iceberg might tell her little polar bears, "The world is all snow and ice—just a huge refrigerator; I've been everywhere and I know."

A bear in the woods might tell her little bear cubs, "The world is all woods—just a huge forest; I've been everywhere and I know."

In the same way people used to tell their little children, "The world is just a big island like a huge mud pie with some water, some sand, some ice, and some trees on it, and with a cover we call the sky over us all; we've been everywhere and we know."

---

left: The planet Earth in the Universe

When some inquisitive child asked, "What does the flat world like a mud pie rest on?" they said, "It rests on the backs of four elephants."

But when the inquisitive child asked, "And what do the elephants stand on?" they said, "On a big turtle."

Then when the inquisitive child asked, "What does the turtle stand on?" no one could say, for no one could even guess farther than that.

That's the old story that parents long ago used to tell their children about what the world was like. But today, of course, we know much more about the world than that.

The world from way off in space looks something like a full moon—round and very bright—for the sun shines on this big ball, our world, Earth, and makes it light just as the headlights on an automobile shine on the road at night and make the road light. Of course, the sun can shine on only one side of this big ball at a time; the other side of the world is dark, but the world keeps turning round and round in the sunlight.

If you looked at the world through a telescope, as men look at the moon, you would see on one side of the world two big patches that look like shadows; and on the other side of the world, four shadows. These shadows are land and are called continents. The continents have names: North America, South America, Europe, Asia, Africa, Australia, and Antarctica.

We call one side of the world the *western hemisphere* and the other side the *eastern hemisphere*. Hemisphere means "half a ball." The western hemisphere has two continents and the eastern hemisphere has four continents. Antarctica is in both hemispheres.

The very top and the very bottom of the world are called the *poles*. Around the top and bottom pole it is white, for the poles are so cold that there is snow and ice there all the time.

The part of the world that isn't land is water. The water all around the continents is the ocean, and its different parts are called by different names.

The Atlantic Ocean is on the east side of North and South America. The Pacific Ocean is on the west. The ocean entirely in the eastern hemisphere is called the Indian Ocean. At the top of the world is the Arctic Ocean. At the bottom, all around Antarctica, is the Antarctic Ocean. The Arctic and Antarctic Oceans are mostly ice, for it is so cold there the water freezes and stays frozen.

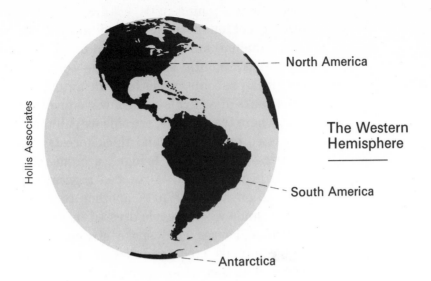

North America

The Western
Hemisphere
————

South America

Antarctica

Hollis Associates

There is no reason why I should show you the world turned with North America on top. I might just as well show it upside down or sideways, for there is no upside nor downside on the world. I suppose the reason the north side is always shown on top is because the people who made maps and geographies all lived in the north part of the world and they wanted their part of the world on top.

So this is our world. You may wonder, "Are there any other worlds besides ours?" Some have guessed that there may be—that some of those sparks in the sky that look like stars at night may be other planets like ours and that there may be people living on them. But no one knows yet, though we are learning more about these planets every day.

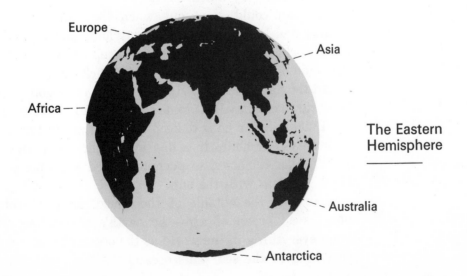

Europe

Asia

Africa

The Eastern
Hemisphere
————

Australia

Antarctica

The Surface of the Earth

When I was a young man, I started out to go around the world. I got on a train headed toward the setting sun. Night came on, but I kept on and on, day after day, week after week, month after month—sometimes on trains, sometimes on boats, sometimes in automobiles, sometimes on the backs of animals—but always toward the side of the world where the sun sets, the side we call the West.

I passed broad fields and thick forests, small towns and big cities—I went over bridges, around hills, and through tunnels in mountains—I reached a great ocean and sailed across it on a big ship to another continent—I came to strange lands where people dressed in strange clothes, lived in strange houses, and spoke strange languages; I saw strange animals, trees, and flowers; I crossed another great ocean and at last, after many, many months, always going in the same direction, I came back to the exact spot from which I had started.

It took me nearly half a year to go around the world. That is a long time, but it was a long way—over twenty-five times a thousand miles. But others have been around the world in much faster time.

If you boarded a jet passenger plane in New York and went around the world, you would have to stop at many different airports and change planes. You might take a plane from New York to San Francisco and then change planes. The next plane might take you to Hawaii, then you might go to Japan, then India, Turkey, France, and finally back to New York. This could take about sixty hours—less than three days. But you would see nothing but airports. You wouldn't see much land because jet planes go too high for you to see very much.

If a man could start out when the sun rose in the morning and keep up with it all day long, go over the side of the world when the sun set, and keep up with it on the other side of the world, he would be back again where he started the next morning. He then would have gone around the world in one day. But to do that he would have to travel over 1,000 miles an hour to keep up with the sun for each of the twenty-four hours in a day and night. Jet planes now fly 600 miles an hour, so perhaps someday people will be able to keep up with the sun.

All around the outside of the world, as you probably know, is an ocean of air—the earth's atmosphere—that covers everything in the world as the ocean of water covers everything in the sea. This ocean of air is wrapped only

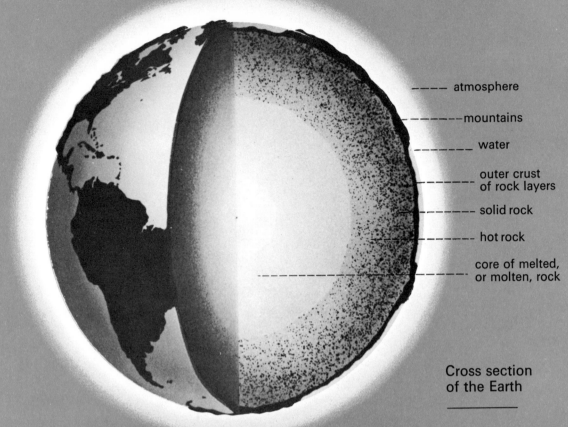

— — — atmosphere

— — — — mountains

— — — — water

outer crust
of rock layers

— — — solid rock

— — — hot rock

core of melted,
or molten, rock

**Cross section
of the Earth**

——————

round the world—it does not fill the sky. Men and animals
live in this ocean of air as fish live in the ocean of water,
and if you left this atmosphere without wearing a space
suit supplied with an artificial atmosphere you would die
just as quickly as a fish does when taken out of the sea. The
air is thick near the ground but gets thinner and thinner
the higher up you go off the ground. That's why airplanes
can go up only a few miles high—there is not enough air to
hold up the plane, for the plane must have air to rest on and
for its propeller to push against, just as a boat in the water
must have water to rest on and water for its propeller to
push against. Or if it's a jet plane, it must have air to feed
its jet motors. An airplane could not rise beyond the ocean
of air and sail off into the sky where there is no air any
more than a steamship on the sea could rise out of the
water and sail off up into the air.

There is only one thing that men can send up high
enough to travel above the ocean of air. That is a rocket,

which doesn't depend on air for its motor or to hold it up. Someday very, very soon rocket ships will carry men on trips to the moon or even to the planet Mars. How would you like to go exploring in a rocket ship beyond the world's atmosphere out through airless space? How would you like to be the first man on the moon? You wouldn't find any living thing on the moon, for the moon is a dead, lifeless ball without any air on it at all. But if your rocket got to Mars you might very well find some living plants or animals.

Some mountains on earth are so high that their tops almost stick out of the ocean of air; at least, there is so little air covering their tops that people can't go all the way to the top unless they take along oxygen.

You can't see air. You may think you can see it, but what you see is smoke or clouds, not air. When air is moving, we call it wind. Then you can feel it when it blows your hat off, you can hear it when it bangs the shutters and whistles around the house; but you can't see it.

The world wasn't always the same as it is now. It was once a ball of fire—a huge burning ball. That was millions of years ago, and of course long before there were any people or animals or plants on the world. But the fiery ball got cooler and cooler until it was no longer burning but a hot ball of rock. Clouds of steam formed around the world. But the world kept getting cooler and cooler until at last the steam turned to water and fell on the world—rain, rain, rain, until there perhaps was one big ocean covering the whole world.

But the world still kept on cooling and cooling, and as it cooled it shrank and shriveled and wrinkled and crinkled and puckered like the outside of a prune. These little wrinkles and crinkles rose up out of the ocean and were the continents and mountains, so you see how big the wrinkles and crinkles really are. The earth is still wrinkling a bit even now, and when it does so it shivers and shakes and we say there has been an earthquake. We know the continents rose out of the water because we can find seashells on the tops of high mountains, and we know they could have been made only under the water when the mountain was under the water.

The earth as it may have looked
millions of years ago—
a burning ball of fire

Below the Surface

It is eight thousand miles straight through the earth and most of the way is rock—just rock, and more rock, that's all.

How do we know it's eight thousand miles if no one has ever been through the world? We know because every ball, whether it is a little ball or a medium-sized ball or a great big ball, is always just a little more than three times as big around as it is through.

We know the world is a ball, a huge ball, and since it is a ball it must, like all other balls, be a little more than three times as big around as it is through. It is twenty-five thousand miles around the world, so we know that the distance through must be about eight thousand miles, for twenty-five is a little more than three times eight.

The outside of the world is a crust of rock like the skin of a baked potato over the hot inside. Some of the crust that you go through first is in layers, one layer after another. These rock layers are made of sand and shells, or coal or little stones. If you could cut the world in half as if it were an apple, we would have a *cross section*.

Between some of the layers of rock there is coal and in other places there are gold and silver and diamonds and rubies, and in some of the rock there are pools of oil. That's why men dig wells down through these layers of rock to get oil, and that's why men dig mines to get coal and gold.

And still farther down the rock is not in layers—it is just solid rock; and still farther down it gets hotter and hotter where the earth has not cooled off yet, until the rock is no longer solid, but melted.

Whenever you see a chimney you know there is a furnace beneath it, and when smoke and fire come out of its top you know there is a fire in the furnace. There are many places in the world where fire and smoke come out of the ground as if through a chimney from a fiery furnace. These places are called volcanoes.

Hawaii Visitors Bureau Photo

right: An eruption of the Kilauea Volcano, one of the two active volcanoes on the island of Hawaii. It has been called "the drive-in volcano" because people may drive to the rim for a good view of the bubbling inferno below.

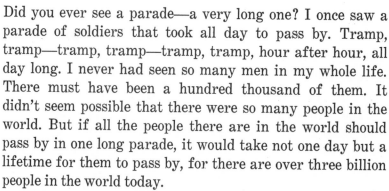

The People who Live in the World

Did you ever see a parade—a very long one? I once saw a parade of soldiers that took all day to pass by. Tramp, tramp—tramp, tramp—tramp, tramp, hour after hour, all day long. I never had seen so many men in my whole life. There must have been a hundred thousand of them. It didn't seem possible that there were so many people in the world. But if all the people there are in the world should pass by in one long parade, it would take not one day but a lifetime for them to pass by, for there are over three billion people in the world today.

Babies are born every minute of the day and night; many are born while you are reading this, and with every tick of the clock someone has died. But more people are born than die each day, so that the world is getting fuller and fuller of people all the time. It is predicted that there will be about *six billion* people in the world by the year 2000—about *twice* as many as there are now!

The people in the world are all about the same size and shape. They all have one head, one nose, one mouth; they all have two ears, two eyes, two arms, and two legs. And yet in

22

all these billions of people there are no two alike, there is not a single person exactly like any other one. Even twins are not exactly alike.

The noticeable differences in people are the color of their hair, their facial features, and the color of their skin. With films, television, photography and transportation, very few people today are ignorant of the many different types in the world today. In many parts of the world there are people who are a mixture of races because of explorers and settlers. The important thing is not the color of a person's skin or whether he has straight or curly hair, but the country to which he belongs. A person does not salute a flag that belongs to a certain race, but a flag that belongs to a country that he loves and respects.

There are only six continents where people live, but on most of these there are several countries. *A* country doesn't mean *the* country. *A* country means cities, towns, villages, and country under one leader. At this writing there are 130 countries in the world. As we have mentioned, the population of the world is about three billion. Some countries are small, with only a few thousand people in the whole country, and some countries are large with many millions of people. The United States, has about 190 million people, but there are several countries with more. China, which is on the other side of the world has about 700 million people. India, another country on the other side of the world from the United States, has the next largest number of people. Both these countries are in Asia—the largest continent with the shortest name and the most people.

Each country has a leader, just as every ball team has a captain. Some countries have a king for a leader and some have a president. Most countries have other people to help govern with the king or the president. Some countries have a dictator who really rules alone.

United Nations

Pacific Area Travel
Association Photo

UNATIONS

A king is a king because his father was a king, and his son will be king for the same reason. A president is president because he was chosen by the people in the country, just as the captain of a team is chosen by the members of his team. Choosing we call *voting*. A king is king for his whole life, but a president is president for only a few years.

The country of a king is called a kingdom. If one man rules over several countries, he is sometimes called an emperor and the countries together are called an empire. A country in which every person has a direct voice in the government is called a republic. The people in a republic elect men called representatives to carry out their wishes. The king or the president and the others who are elected make up the government. The government makes the rules, but it also does two things that no one else is allowed to do. It makes the money and the postage stamps of the country.

The people of the world speak many different languages. Even in the same country many different languages are spoken. There are over 3,000 different languages! You probably speak only one of these, and couldn't talk to anyone nor understand anyone who spoke any other language than your own. In the United States almost everyone speaks English, which is also the language of another country—England. But on a continent like Europe you could hardly go a day's journey without hearing a different language on the street, in the shops, at the hotel.

If you happened to be born in the United States or England, and heard everybody around you speaking English, you would learn to speak English too. But if you had been born in Asia, you would learn to speak Chinese or an Indian dialect or maybe Japanese. If you had been born in Africa, you would learn an African dialect.

Some people know how to speak many different languages. You can understand how wonderful this is when you realize that it usually takes years to learn to speak *one* other language besides your own.

The letters of the alphabets of many of these different languages are the same; they are called Roman, because a people called Romans first used them long ago. But the letters of Greek, Russians, Chinese, and Japanese and some other languages are different from the Roman letters.

Consulate of Japan

UNESCO/Eric Schwab

UNATIONS

UNESCO/Eric Schwab, 1952

UNRWA

The United States of America

The continents of North and South America are named after an Italian navigator who lived in the time of Columbus. He believed, because of his studies and travels, that the land Columbus had discovered was a New World—not part of Asia, as Columbus thought. His name was Amerigo Vespucci.

Have you ever seen a buffalo nickel from the United States of America? On the head side is the picture of an Indian with feathers in his hair. Why do you suppose the United States has the picture of an Indian on the nickel? On the tail side is the picture of a buffalo. Why do you suppose the United States has a picture of a buffalo on the nickel instead of a horse or a cow?

Well, long before there were any settlers, or any horses or cows, there were a great many Indians and a great many buffaloes in the United States. Now there are very few Indians and very few buffaloes in America, so these pictures on the nickel were to remind people that the Indian was the first American man and the buffalo was the first American animal.

If you will look at the printing on the nickel you will see it says "United States of America." That's the full name of the country, but it is too long to say United States of America every time, so we usually say United States or America or use just the initials U.S.A.

Have you ever seen a picture of a tall man with a suit of clothes that looked as if it had been made out of a flag, with red and white striped pants, a long-tailed coat, and a tall hat with stars on it? There never was such a man really, but he is supposed to be the symbol of the United States. As the initials of the United States are U.S., someone said they stand for Uncle Sam, so the man dressed in a flag is called Uncle Sam.

The map of the United States looks as if it were made like a patchwork quilt. The patches are different sizes and shapes. These patches are the states that are united—that means, joined to one another. As a matter of fact, of course, there are no lines between the states. The lines on the map

Buffalo nickel,
Indian head side

Buffalo nickel,
Buffalo side

The United States and its Possessions

left: This view of the globe shows the western hemisphere, with North America at the top. Land masses are shown in darker color; the United States, Puerto Rico, and the Hawaiian Islands are shown in black.

---

below: The United States of America

---

bottom of page: An enlargement of Alaska, the Hawaiian Islands, and Puerto Rico. To see their geographical locations, look at the globe at the top of the page.

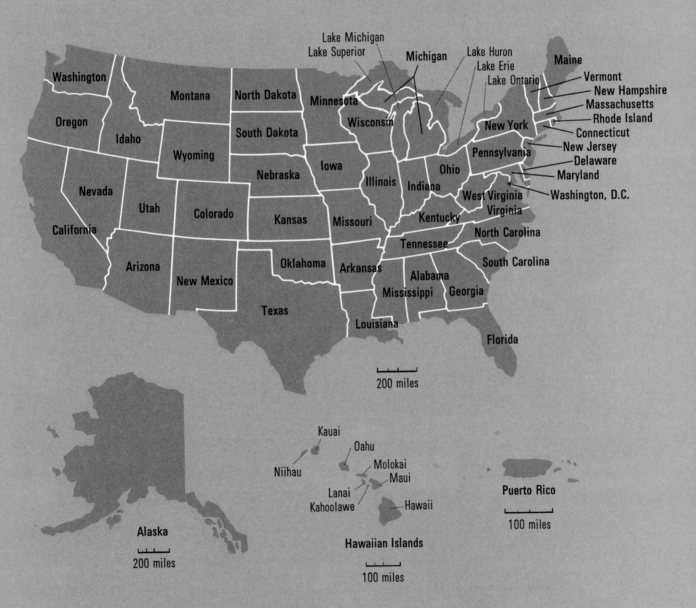

Lake Michigan
Lake Superior
Michigan
Lake Huron
Lake Erie
Lake Ontario
Maine
Vermont
New Hampshire
Massachusetts
Rhode Island
Connecticut
New Jersey
Delaware
Maryland
Washington, D.C.

Washington
Montana
North Dakota
Minnesota
Oregon
Idaho
South Dakota
Wisconsin
New York
Pennsylvania
Wyoming
Iowa
Ohio
Nevada
Utah
Colorado
Nebraska
Illinois
Indiana
West Virginia
Virginia
California
Kansas
Missouri
Kentucky
North Carolina
Arizona
Oklahoma
Arkansas
Tennessee
South Carolina
New Mexico
Alabama
Georgia
Mississippi
Texas
Louisiana
Florida

200 miles

Alaska
200 miles

Kauai
Oahu
Niihau
Molokai
Maui
Lanai
Kahoolawe
Hawaii
Hawaiian Islands
100 miles

Puerto Rico
100 miles

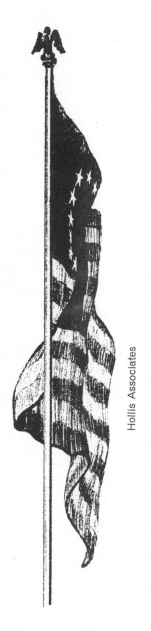

Hollis Associates

The thirteen-star flag of the original thirteen states

are marked on the ground by stone posts set so far apart that it is possible to cross from one state to another without even knowing when you are in a different state. There are signs, however, on most of the well-traveled highways that tell you when you are crossing from one state to another. Each state has towns and cities and country. Everyone in the United States must live in some state unless—I'll tell you later the few places he may live without being in any state.

Some of the states have straight sides and some have one, two, or more crooked sides. Some are big and some are little. The biggest state is Alaska, at the far upper left-hand corner beside Canada. This is the northwestern corner of the North American Continent. The smallest state is Rhode Island, which is not an island at all. It is near the upper right-hand corner, in the northeast.

Not so long ago there was no United States. There were only thirteen little states along the shore of the Atlantic Ocean. These states were so small they thought they ought to form a club. There is an old story about a man who wanted to break a bundle of sticks. He tried and he tried but he couldn't break the bundle. Then someone told him to take the bundle apart and break each stick separately; so he did, and broke them easily. The states thought that they, in the same way, might be broken easily if they remained separate, so they tied themselves together like a bundle of sticks in order that they might not be "broken" by an enemy. And so the thirteen states formed the United States. They took as their motto "In Union is Strength."

Now thirteen is generally considered an unlucky number, but these thirteen states were not afraid of bad luck.

In fact, as the new country had to have a flag, they made a flag with thirteen stripes—seven red stripes and six white—and they put a white star for each state in a blue corner of the flag. Other parts of North America thought they'd like to join the union too, and more and more states joined until by 1959 there were fifty states. These states that were united stretched from the Atlantic Ocean on one side to the middle of the Pacific Ocean on the other—that is, from where the sun rises from the ocean on one side to where it sets over the ocean on the other. Each time a state joined the United States another star was put in the corner of the flag, but the number of stripes was not changed, for the thirteen stripes stand for the original thirteen colonies. Now there are fifty stars—that means fifty states united into one country. That's why there are on American coins the words *e pluribus unum*, which means "one from many."

Not all of North America joined the club, however. The country north of the United States called Canada and the country south of the United States called Mexico did not join. And yet the people in Canada are Americans, and the people in Mexico are Americans too, but both Canada and Mexico have different leaders, for they are different countries.

Indian names are used for some of the states. See if you can pick out some of the states on the map that have Indian names. Maryland and Virginia, of course, are not Indian names—they are girls' names. States beginning with "New"—like New York, New Jersey, New Hampshire— are named after old places in another country. But Minnesota, which means "sky blue water;" Ohio, which means "beautiful river" or "great;" and many others *are* Indian.

Cherry blossoms around the Tidal Basin in Washington, D.C. The Jefferson Memorial is in the background.

Washington, District of Columbia

When the thirteen American colonies became a country, men tried to find a suitable place for the capital. Eight places were tried out and at last a swamp was chosen as the proper place to build the city, because it was then near the center of the country. So the swamp was drained and a city was built there called Washington after George Washington, the first President of the United States. It is now one of the most beautiful cities in the world, with lovely parks and beautiful buildings. George Washington didn't live in Washington. He lived in Virginia, fifteen miles away, at a placed called Mount Vernon. Washington is now near the edge of the United States. The capital hasn't moved, but the center of the country has.

There are many cities in the United States named "Washington." Washington, the capital, looks on the map as if it were in the state of Maryland, but it isn't. It isn't in any state. The capital of all the states had to have a place all its own; so this piece of land is called the District of Columbia, or D.C. for short. The District of Columbia is named after Columbus, the man who discovered America. So if you write a letter to anyone in Washington, the capital, you must be very careful to put "D.C." after Washington, for there are so many cities and towns named Washington that your letter might not go to the right one.

When I was a boy I thought the Capitol was the most beautiful building in the world. I used to climb to the top of the dome—for there was no elevator—to see the view of the city, and to look down on the inside at the floor far below where people walking seemed like ants crawling.

On one side of the Capitol is a large room called the *Senate*, and on the other side is a still larger room called the *House of Representatives*. The men who sit at desks in both the Senate and the House of Representatives are the men who make the laws that govern all the people in all the states of the United States. The men in the Senate are called *Senators*. The men in the House are called *Representatives* or *Congressmen*. When we say "men" we mean women, too, for some of the Senators and Representatives are women.

Each state chooses two Senators to go to the Capitol in Washington. No matter whether the state is big like Texas or whether it is little like Rhode Island, it sends only two

U.S. Capitol, Washington, D.C.

right: The White House,
Washington, D.C.

Senators. Each state also sends to the Capitol in Washington other men or women called Representatives, but the number of Representatives each state sends depends on the number of people in the state; New York has the most people, so it sends the greatest number of Representatives. Several states, including Nevada, have so few people that they send only one Representative. The Senate and the House of Representatives together are called *Congress*, and when Congress is in session a flag flies over the Capitol.

Look in the front of this book or any other book and you will see printed there a notice called a *Copyright*. Just across a park from the Capitol is a large building with a golden dome on top. This building is the Library of Congress. Everyone in the United States who prints a book sends two copies of it to this library, and the library sends him a "copy right," which means that no one else has the "right" to copy it or print it without his permission. In the Library of Congress there are more books than in any other building in the United States.

Look on a camera or record player, or any other machine in your home, and see if you can find the word *Patented*. Anyone in the United States who invents anything new and useful, whether it is a fountain pen, an airplane, or a mousetrap, sends one—a model, it is called—to another building in Washington called the Patent Office and asks for a patent. If the thing is really new and no one has ever made anything of the kind before, the Patent Office gives him the sole right to make and sell it, and no one else is allowed to make or sell it. That is called a patent.

Some of the greatest parades have passed down a very wide street in Washington called Pennsylvania Avenue, or usually just "The Avenue." It might be called "Parade Avenue." It stretches from the Capitol to another building about a mile away called the Treasury. There is a picture of the Treasury on the $10 bill. In this building is kept money of the United States.

Paper money and postage stamps are printed in another building.

The money made of silver, nickel, and copper is made in places called *Mints*.

In Washington there is a large museum called the Smithsonian Institution in which there is a huge collection of all sorts of curious and remarkable things from all over the world.

There are many white houses in the United States, but next door to the Treasury is a white house that is different from any other, for the President lives in this house. There is a picture of it on the $20 bill. From the back porch of the White House the latest President of the United States can look across his back yard and see a monument to the First President—Washington. The Washington Monument is like a giant spire, five hundred and fifty-five feet high— about a tenth of a mile high.

There is a long pool of water at the foot of the Washington Monument in which you can see the monument reflected the way it would be reflected in a mirror. At the other end of this pool is a marble building with columns all around the four sides. It was built in honor of Abraham Lincoln, the sixteenth President. There is a picture of Lincoln on the $5 bill and on the other side a picture of the Lincoln Memorial. Lincoln was born in a very small house made of logs. He was very poor as a boy, and yet he became President of the United States. While he was President two sections of the United States fought a terrible war with each other—the Civil War—and almost became un-united, but Lincoln kept the states together. That's one of the main reasons why this beautiful building was built in his honor. The only thing in the building is a statue of Lincoln sitting in a chair. He looks down on the crowds of people who visit him, as if his spirit were inside that figure of stone.

right: The Washington Monument, Washington, D.C.

American Airlines

Fort McHenry, Baltimore, Maryland, Birthplace of "The Star Spangled Banner" written by Francis Scott Key in September, 1814.

Loading oysters in Chesapeake Bay

Maryland, Virginia, and Pennsylvania

Long before there was any Washington or any United States there were trader Indians living on the shores of the river that flows by Washington. These Indians paddled their canoes up and down the river and traded with other Indians, swapping things they had for things they wanted —beads for furs, bows for arrows, corn for potatoes. In the Indian language the name for traders was potomac, so we call the river after these trader Indians, the Potomac River. The Potomac separates two states—Maryland and Virginia. They are named after two queens. The Potomac Indians paddled their canoes down the river until they came to a much broader body of water. This body of water was so big it seemed to them like the ocean, and they called it "the Mother of Waters," which in their own language was "Chesapeake." Chesapeake Bay is not the ocean, but it is the biggest bay in the United States.

The Indians found oysters growing in the Chesapeake Bay. At first no one thought of eating oysters—they didn't look good to eat. But one day an Indian who was very hungry broke open an oyster shell and ate the oyster inside. It tasted good and it didn't hurt him, so others began to eat oysters, and now almost everyone likes oysters, either raw or cooked. Oysters grow in other parts of the world too, but many people say that those in the Chesapeake Bay are the largest and best.

Near Chesapeake Bay are two cities. One is named Annapolis. The other is named Baltimore. Annapolis means Anna's City, and it too was named after a queen. That makes three places—Anna's City, Mary's Land, and Virginia's State—named after queens. Annapolis is the capital of the state of Maryland, just as Washington is the capital of all the states. At Annapolis the United States has a school called the Naval Academy. Boys chosen from each state in the United States go to Annapolis. They study all about ships and naval warfare and about geography; they visit other countries and learn to command ships.

Baltimore is the largest city in Maryland. It was named after an English lord. The first railroad in America started in Baltimore, and as it ran from Baltimore to the state of Ohio, it was called the Baltimore & Ohio, or the B. & O. for short. Baltimore is famous for the Johns Hopkins University and Hospital. Young men come from all over the world to study there and people come from all over the world to be treated there.

A man named Penn once owned the state just north of Maryland. It was then all woods, so it was called Pennsylvania, which means Penn's Woods. But ages before Penn's Woods grew there other woods were there—huge forests of trees and giant plants growing high and thick. Ages passed and these forests died and became buried and mashed down under the ground and turned into black rock. More ages passed and men dug up this black rock, and by accident they found that unlike other rock this rock would burn. It would burn because it was coal.

There are two kinds of coal. One is called hard coal, or *anthracite*, and the other is called soft coal, or *bituminous*. Soft coal crumbles easily. Hard coal is better. Soft coal is dirtier and smokier, but is much less expensive than hard coal. In the eastern part of Pennsylvania the coal that comes out of the ground is hard; in the western part it is soft.

Men called miners work underneath the ground, where it is like night all day long, digging out coal to be used for fuel. They have been digging away for years and years, so that there are huge hollow places underneath parts of Pennsylvania.

Coal is in layers underneath the ground and between layers of rock. There are also iron mines in Pennsylvania, and iron is not in layers; it is all mixed through the rock under the ground and is called *ore*. To get the iron out of the ore, men build huge fires under the ore and the iron melts and runs out, like water, into troughs which they make in the ground to catch it. When the iron cools, the blocks of iron are called "pigs."

opposite, top: Ironworks, Pennsylvania. In a blast furnace department, molten iron runs into ladles built on railroad cars (known as "submarine" ladle cars) and is transported to the steelmaking departments.

opposite, bottom: Coal miners in electrically operated cage at Grassy Island

To get iron out of iron ore you must have heat, and to have heat you must have something to make heat with, like coal. Some places have iron ore but no fuel, and some places have fuel but no iron. But Pittsburgh, in the western part of Pennsylvania, has both iron and coal nearby.

From the ore they make iron, and from the iron they make steel, and from the steel they make rails for railroad tracks and beams for tall buildings and bridges to cross rivers.

Philadelphia means the City of Brotherly Love. This name was chosen for the largest city in Pennsylvania—in fact, the fourth largest city in all the United States. Philadelphia was the capital of the United States before there was any Washington, D.C. Here in an old building called Independence Hall is the bell that rang out the news when the United States was first made a country. It is now cracked, so will not ring any more, but is more treasured than any bell in the United States that can ring.

right: Independence Hall, Philadelphia, Pennsylvania, where the Declaration of Independence was signed and the Constitution of the United States was debated and adopted.

The Empire State

Several countries together are called an *Empire*. New York State is called the Empire State, because it has as many people, who do as much business and make as much money, as several countries put together.

Down at the southeast corner of New York State is New York City, one of the four largest cities in the world. There are more tall buildings in New York City than anywhere else in the world. It is the city of millionaires and of millions who are not. People from all over the world come to New York hoping to be millionaires too. Some used to think the streets were paved with gold, and were disappointed when they found them just asphalt.

The main part of New York City is on an island that the Indians called Manhattan. Early settlers bought it from the Indians and paid them about $24 for the whole island. That is, they paid them in beads and ornaments worth $24. A piece of ground only large enough to stand on would now cost many times more than what the whole island once cost. That may seem a big price for a small piece of ground, but a plot of ground can be a very valuable thing. In New York City land is now very scarce and very expensive. In New York men build buildings up to the sky—skyscrapers—for a fifty-story building takes up no more land than a one-story building.

To me there is nothing in the world made by the hand of man more wonderful than New York's giant buildings. They stand unmoved by thunder and lightning, by wind, storm, or tempest. New York's motto is "Excelsior," which means "Higher," and that is the motto of its builders. One of the greatest of these buildings—sixty stories high—was built from the nickels and dimes made by Woolworth's Five and Ten Cent Stores. The most marvelous building of all is called the Empire State Building. It is one hundred and two stories high!

left: New York City at night

right: The Empire State Building towers above its neighbors in Midtown Manhattan

United Air Lines

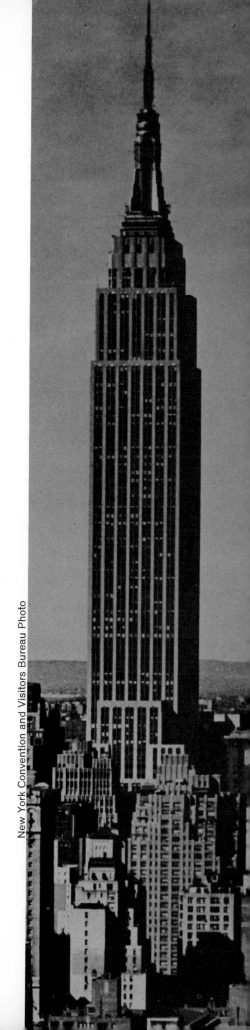

New York Convention and Visitors Bureau Photo

Aerial view of some
New York City skyscrapers

One group of high buildings in New York might be called the capitol of the world. After World War II most of the countries of the world wanted to find some way of keeping a third World War from happening. These countries each send men to meet together in the same way American states send men to Congress. At their meetings they discuss matters that are of interest to all the countries of the world. When any country quarrels with another these people try to have them settle their quarrel without fighting. This congress is called the United Nations or in short form, the U.N. The United Nations decided that New York City would be the best place to have its meetings and carry on its business. So there its offices were built. When the buildings were dedicated, or solemnly set apart for United Nations use, the speeches were broadcast in twenty-six different languages.

At a meeting of the United Nations each speaker speaks in one of the official languages of the U.N. yet he can be understood by all the other people there, for everyone wears earphones and hears a translation of the speech in the language he understands. There are five official languages in the U.N.—French, English, Russian, Spanish, and Chinese. Of course the people who do the translation must know at least two languages, for they have to listen in one language and speak into a microphone in another language. What they speak into the microphones is what is heard in the earphones. Millions of other people watch the United Nations meetings on television.

On a little island in New York Harbor is a huge bronze statue called the Goddess of Liberty. She holds a torch in her upraised hand. Her hand is over sixteen feet long. One finger is eight feet long. Her nose is four and one-half feet long. Her mouth is a yard wide. You can climb up on the inside into the Goddess's head and arm, and a dozen people can stand inside her torch. She was given to all the people of the United States by the people of France.

On one side of Manhattan Island is the Hudson River and on the other side is the East River. A bridge was built across the East River by stretching ropes made of steel from one side of the river to the other and hanging the floor of the bridge from these steel ropes. This is called a suspension bridge. It is called the Brooklyn Bridge because at the other end of it on Long Island is the part of New York City called Brooklyn. Brooklyn Bridge was the first big, long bridge built this way. It is suspended in the air so high

above: The Brooklyn Bridge

right: The United Nations Secretariat Building

below: New York Harbor

above: The Holland Tunnel

---

top right: Fifth Avenue, New York

---

middle right: Times Square at night
looking north along Seventh Avenue
from 47th Street toward Broadway

---

bottom right: Waldman Memorial
Rink, Central Park, New York

above the water that even now the greatest ships easily pass beneath it.

Other bridges have been built over the East River and the Hudson River to New York City. The world's largest suspension bridge is the Verrazzano-Narrows Bridge. It goes from Brooklyn to Staten Island. Staten Island is a very big island in New York Harbor, near New Jersey. Also, tunnels for cars have been dug *under* the Hudson River and the East River.

Three of the most famous streets in the world are in Manhattan. A part of Broadway is lighted so brightly at night by thousands of electric lights and flashing electric signs that it is often called "The Great White Way." Fifth Avenue is a famous street with many of the finest and most expensive shops on it. Seventh Avenue is known all over the world because on and around only four blocks most of the dresses and coats worn by American women and children are made. Most of the people travel from their homes to their work or school by trains that run in tubes underground. These underground tubes are called subways.

Although land in New York City is worth more than any other land in the world, there are three famous big parks where city people enjoy trees and grass. Central Park is fifty blocks long and several blocks wide, and Bronx Park has a wonderful zoo. Prospect Park in Brooklyn has a renowned Botanical Garden and a museum.

On the west edge of New York State are two great lakes with Indian names—Lake Erie and Lake Ontario. Lake Erie on the map looks lower than Lake Ontario, but it is really much higher. So the water from Lake Erie falls over a high and broad cliff to reach Lake Ontario. This waterfall is called Niagara, and though there are other falls in the world higher and other falls broader, Niagara is one of the most beautiful and famous, and people go from all over the world to see it. The roar of the water as it thunders over the edge can be heard for miles, and when the sun is shining there is a rainbow in the spray that rises from the bottom of the falls. Thousands of people view the falls each day.

New York Convention and Visitors Bureau Photo

right: A herd of Nyala antelopes on the African Plains of the Bronx Zoo.

47

American Airlines

A part of Niagara is caught in a huge bucket as it falls, and the falling water turns giant wheels in the bottom of the bucket. The wheels make electricity, which is carried on wires to turn the wheels of mills, to light the houses and streets in the city of Buffalo nearby, and other places farther away.

Boats on Lake Erie that wanted to go to Lake Ontario couldn't jump the falls. So men dug a river around Niagara Falls from Lake Erie to Lake Ontario and put water steps in it so that boats could go downhill to Lake Ontario or uphill to Lake Erie. This man-made river is called the Welland Canal.

It may seem strange for a boat to step downhill, but it not only can step downhill, it can step uphill too. A water step down a hill is called a "lock." If a boat wants to go downhill it moves into the lock. The gate is closed behind it. The water in the lock is then let out and the boat lowers as the water lowers. When the boat is at the right level, doors at the end of the lock are opened and the boat moves out on the lower canal. If a boat wants to go uphill it moves into the bottom of the lock through the open doors, the doors are then closed, and the water is turned on. As it fills the lock the boat rises with it, for water will lift anything that will float, whether it is the smallest ship or the biggest ship. Water has more power to lift and lower the largest steamship than even giant machinery would have. It lifts the largest battleship as easily and softly as it would the lightest feather floating on the surface—as easily as you might lift a snowflake on your hand.

Boats that wanted to go to New York City once had to go down through the Welland Canal and locks to Lake Ontario, then all the way out the St. Lawrence River, which runs from Lake Ontario to the Atlantic Ocean, then go down the coast to New York. To avoid this long detour, this long way around, men dug a canal all the way across New York State from Buffalo on Lake Erie to the Hudson River, so that big boats can now cut across from Lake Erie to New York City. This is called the Barge Canal. It's one of the longest canals in the world.

left: Niagara Falls, New York

The New England States

About 300 years ago people came from England to the northeast corner of the United States and made their homes there. So the six states north of New York, where they settled, are called New England. The Indians tried to call the white people "English," but the best they could say was "Yenghees" or "Yankees." The people of New England are still called "Yankees." All six states of New England could be put in any one of several states in the West; but though the New England states are small in size, they are big in many other things.

New England in winter is very cold; the land is so rocky that men make their fences of stones gathered from the fields. The cold and the rocks make it very hard to grow things there, but there are many, many waterfalls in New England, and waterfalls can be used to turn the wheels of factories to make things, so the main thing people do in New England is make things for the rest of the United States—thousands of different kinds of things—not big things such as railroad tracks and bridges that they make in Pittsburgh, but small things such as needles and pins, watches and clocks, boots and shoes. If the wheels of the factories are turned by waterfalls they are called *mills*. Nowadays, most of the waterfalls are used to make electricity, and the electricity is used to run the machinery, but the factories are still called mills.

One of the things made in these New England mills is shoes. In New England enough shoes are made for every pair of feet in the United States. Shoes wear out, so we can understand why the mills keep on, year after year, making so many shoes. But in one of the states—Connecticut—pins are made, enough pins for every man, woman and child in the United States to use 100 every year. What becomes of so many pins, do you suppose? They don't wear out like shoes, and yet they disappear—billions of pins every year.

right: A winter scene in New Hampshire

American Airlines

top: A moose in the Maine woods

bottom: A deer in Maine

And clocks and watches—millions of them are made too, though one clock or one watch should last a person a lifetime—little watches for the wrist and little clocks for mantelpieces and big clocks for clock towers.

And spools of thread—enough thread is made in one mill in a single day to wind around the world—that is, over twenty-five thousand miles of thread in one mill in one day!

New England is a vacationland for many people from other parts of the country, because there are so many lakes, waterfalls, and beautiful spots for camps, streams for fishing, and in the Maine woods places for hunting deer and moose. In New Hampshire there are mountains called the White Mountains, and one of these White Mountains, named after the first president, is Mount Washington. It is the highest mountain in this part of the country, and because it is so high many people like to climb it.

In Vermont, which means "green mountain," there are the Green Mountains, not as high as the White Mountains, but very lovely. All along the New England coast are places where people go to spend the summer, because this part of the country is cool while the rest of the country is hot.

New England is proudest of its schools and colleges. Two of the most noted colleges in the country are in New England—Yale in Connecticut and Harvard in Massachusetts. Harvard is the oldest college in the United States.

Sticking out from Massachusetts like a long, bent finger, as if beckoning to people across the water to come to Massachusetts, is a section of land called Cape Cod. It was named in honor of the codfish, because codfish are so plentiful in those waters. They are caught and dried in great quantities and shipped everywhere.

The finger of Cape Cod has beckoned to people of other lands than England. People who speak many different languages have come to New England to work in factories and mills, so that now almost one quarter of the people in New England are not from England but from many other countries. They are not Yankees, but they have become Americans.

opposite, top: A Vermont farm with Camel's Hump Mountain in the background

opposite, bottom: An art class in Provincetown, Massachusetts, with fishing boats in the background

The Great Lakes

There are five big bodies of water along the northern edge of the United States. They look as if a giant had left his wet umbrella standing and the water had trickled out over the land. We call these bodies of water *The Great Lakes*. Two of the lakes—the smallest two—I have already told you about. They are Lake Erie and Lake Ontario. Two of the others also have Indian names, Lake Michigan, which means "Great Lake," and Lake Huron. The greatest lake of all the Great Lakes is Lake Superior, which means "Greater Lake." Lake Michigan is the only one of the Great Lakes that belongs entirely to the United States, as it is entirely inside of the United States. Half of the other four lakes belong to the country north of the United States—Canada—because these other lakes are along the border between the two countries. The United States owns its side of each of these lakes out to the middle; Canada owns its side out to the middle.

Lake Superior is not only bigger, it is higher than the other lakes. It empties its water into Lake Huron through a little river called St. Mary's. In this river are falls called St. Mary's Jump, because the water jumps—jumps down. These falls are not nearly as high as Niagara Falls, but they are too high for boats to go over the jump, so men had to build canals with locks around the falls to lower boats down and raise them up from one lake to the other. As there are so many boats that want to go down and up, one canal was not enough to take care of all the boats that wanted to go around the falls, so men have built five canals around St. Mary's Jump. St. Mary's Jump in French is Sault Ste. Marie (Soo Saint Marie). People usually call the falls Soo, the river Soo, and the canals Soo too.

right: The greatest commerce in the world moves through the Soo Canal at Sault Ste. Marie. Giant freighters move ore, grain and general cargo from Lake Superior to the industrial cities of the lower lakes and through the St. Lawrence Seaway to foreign ports.

Michigan Tourist Council Photo

54

Some of the boats on the Great Lakes are as big and fine as those on the ocean; they have to be, for the Great Lakes are like small oceans. When you are out, far out, you cannot see land, and at times there are high waves and storms, just as at sea. The chief difference is that the water in the lakes is fresh water, not salt water.

Many people take trips on these big lake boats just as they do on the ocean—for pleasure; but the chief reason for the great number of ships that go from one end of the lakes to the other is not pleasure but business. The business is carrying things, which we call freight. It is much cheaper to send things by ship than by train, for one big ship can carry much more than many trains, and ships do not have to have land and tracks to run on, as trains do.

Eight states are on the Great Lakes, although some of the states have only a small "frontage" on a lake. Michigan has the most frontage, by far. It fronts on four of the Great Lakes, all except Lake Ontario.

You remember that the Potomac Indians were great traders, paddling their canoes up and down the river, and swapping things they had for things they wanted. The Indians of the Great Lakes used to do the same thing. Nowadays huge ships—thousands of times bigger than the Indians' canoes made out of a single log—do the trading. They carry huge loads of freight from one end of the Great Lakes to the other, unloading at different places along the way the things that people want, and loading up with other freight to go back.

Most of the lake ships start at the far end of Lake Superior at a place called Duluth from the wheatlands west of that city, and other trains loaded with iron ore from mines nearby. Then huge machines on the shores of the lakes, with giant hands of iron, lift whole cars of wheat and ore and dump them into the ships waiting to be filled. Other ships collect copper ore and also iron from that part of Michigan which is on Lake Superior. They then carry their loads through the Soo Canal and unload at a city called Detroit, between Lake Huron and Lake Erie, or carry their iron ore to Cleveland and Buffalo on Lake Erie. Most of the ships do not go past Niagara Falls. They load up again with

left: Loading a grain vessel at Duluth

things that have been made in New England, or in the east of the United States, or with coal from Pennsylvania, and go back to Duluth.

Now the cities on the Great Lakes have become seaports. Ocean-going ships now come through the St. Lawrence Seaway into the Great Lakes, bringing cargo from all over the world.

But when winter comes, all this travel up and down the lakes and through the seaway has to stop, for this part of the country is very cold and ice forms and stops the ships.

Most of the automobiles in the world are made in Detroit. Into one end of a Detroit factory go iron and wood, leather, and so on, and out at the other end comes an automobile. Every hour of the day hundreds of automobiles are finished and run out of the factories, to be shipped over the whole world.

The upper part of Michigan is covered with forests of trees especially suited for making furniture, and the manufacture of furniture is one of Michigan's important industries—especially in the city of Grand Rapids. So much furniture is made there that it is often called "the furniture capital of America."

Men have cut down and used most of the original trees in the forests of Michigan, and now they must plant new trees each year to replace the ones they use. This replanting is called *reforestation*.

Side by side, like two children trying to peek out of one small window, are two states looking out on Lake Michigan. They are Illinois and Indiana. The second largest city in the country is in the state of Illinois on the lower end of Lake Michigan. It has an Indian name—Chicago. More

opposite, top: The skyline of Detroit, Michigan

opposite, middle: Aerial view of Ford Motor Company's giant Rouge manufacturing plant in Dearborn, Michigan. It is the only plant on the continent where iron ore, limestone, and coal are unloaded on the docks, smelted into iron, converted into steel, and transformed into engines, frames, bodies, parts, and finally, completed automobiles.

opposite, bottom: Ford Motor Company production line

A section of the
Chicago lakefront
showing in the
foreground Burnham
Harbor and the
Meigs Field airport
and landing strip

trains come into and go out of Chicago than any other city in the world. Most trains going across the United States stop there and start there—freight trains carrying things and passenger trains carrying people. Chicago also has the busiest airport in the world.

Chicago is the world's leading grain center, the producer of more steel than any other city in the country, and the largest commercial printing center.

The city's lakefront is one of the most beautiful in the country. There are public beaches and parks nearly every block of the way, from the southern end of the city to its northern boundary.

Elevated train tracks encircle Chicago's main business district and give it its name—the Loop. In this area are located the famous State Street; the world's busiest intersection; Marshall Field & Company; and some of the many hotels that help make Chicago the convention capital of the world.

Michigan Avenue's "Magnificent Mile," lined with beautiful shops, hotels, and office buildings, extends from the Wrigley Building on the Chicago River to the Old Water Tower, which was one of the few buildings that survived the Chicago Fire of 1871. Just north of the Magnificent Mile is Chicago's Gold Coast, a scenic area of luxury skyscraper apartment buildings overlooking the lakefront.

opposite, top: Chicago and North Western commuter trains at rush hour

opposite, bottom: Navy Pier, Chicago

above: Fly casting in northern Michigan

right: Boys riding their bikes on a forest trail near Harbor Springs, Michigan

American Airlines

opposite: The New York skyline as seen from Brooklyn

right: The Washington Monument at night

below right: El Morro, the Puerto Rican fortress, as seen from the bottom of the bluff on which it stands

below: A covered bridge over the Swift River in Albany, New Hampshire

Photo by Jorge Arroyo

Cypress Gardens in
Winter Haven, Florida

opposite: Pueblo Indian boy at Monument Valley sits near his mother as she weaves

top left: Combine harvesting the wheat crop in western Kansas

bottom left: Pueblo Indians in a horse-drawn wagon at Taos, New Mexico

Drawing by Nita Engle-Hollis Associates

above: Trailriders in the
Grand Canyon

right: Yosemite National Park,
California

72

Dana C. Morgenson

Courtesy of National Cotton Council of America

and animals, and destroys thousands upon thousands of farms and other property.

Near its end, the Mississippi passes the city called New Orleans and at last flows into the Gulf of Mexico. The Mississippi has several mouths, for the water in the river brings along with it so much mud that it settles right in the way of the river's mouth and forms mud islands which the river has to go around, so the river blocks itself.

Where the Mississippi begins in the far north of the United States it is very cold in winter, but as the river flows farther and farther south it gets warmer and warmer and warmer. This warm country is nicknamed "Dixie." When the river is near its end at New Orleans, flowers bloom even at Christmas and it is warm all the year round. This is great cotton-growing land. Strange to say, there was no cotton in America at first. A cotton plant was brought first to Maryland from the other side of the world and grown only for its pretty flowers.

Cotton grows on a low bush in little white balls, and inside each white ball are troublesome little seeds. The cotton is picked off the bush and then these seeds have to be picked out of the cotton before it can be made into cotton thread, and then into cotton cloth, and then into cotton clothes, sheets, towels. Things made of cotton were once very expensive, because it took such a long time to pick the seeds out of the cotton, but a man who was a school teacher invented a way to pick the seeds out by a machine—an "engine" which was called a "gin" for short—and now cotton goods can be made very cheaply. Indeed, it is now hard to understand how we ever got along without cotton, for this little plant that was once grown only for its flowers is used in many ways.

top left: A cotton plant

bottom left: Close-up view of a cotton ball

above: Pirates Alley in the French Quarter of New Orleans

right: A cotton gin

below: Aerial view of the Mississippi Delta at the extreme southeastern tip of Louisiana. This is where the mud forms islands at the river's mouth.

Winter Playground — the State of Florida

Birds go south in the winter to get warm. Some people in the cold northern states do the same. The farthest south they can go in the United States is to the southeast corner state called Florida, which means the land of flowers. On the automobiles that go to Florida you can read the tags of almost every state. People go to Florida in the winter to sit in the sunshine and bathe in the sea. It is a winter playground, as New England is a summer playground.

The first people who came to America came to Florida, because they had been told there was a fountain of youth there. The fountain of youth was supposed to be a spring which was said to have magic powers. It was believed if old people bathed in it or drank its water they would become young again. But no one has ever found a fountain of youth in Florida or anywhere else, though many old people after they have spent the winter in Florida say they *feel* young again.

But not everybody in Florida plays all winter long. Many have to work. They have to run the hotels for the people who do come to Florida to play. And a great many others are busy raising "fresh early vegetables" to ship to the cold northern states, where they would have only canned or frozen vegetables during the winter otherwise. In most of Florida it is so warm that there is seldom frost; fruits and vegetables can be raised the year around. Farmers ship the vegetables they raise out of season to other states, so that people in the North can have fresh strawberries at Christmas, and asparagus too, and lettuce and radishes every month in the year.

The most important fruits from Florida are oranges and grapefruit, which will grow only where there is no frost.

opposite: Beach scene at Clearwater, Florida

Photography by Florida News Bureau, Tallahassee

Grapefruit grows in bunches like big, yellow grapes—that's why it is called grapefruit. Grapefruit was at first thought not fit to eat—too bitter and not sweet like an orange; but people have learned to like it. More grapefruit grows in Florida than in any other place in the world.

Once there was no Florida at all. The sea there was warm and shallow and in the sea there lived millions, billions, trillions of little animals, each like a tiny drop of jelly with a tiny stony speck in the center, or a tiny stony shell on the outside, and millions and billions and trillions of these little sea animals died. As they died, the stony specks and shells fell to the bottom of the sea like a snowfall of chalk dust, and this piled up until the water was filled up. This stony, bony, chalky pile is Florida. On this kind of ground of which Florida is made plants grow very well indeed. In fact, this soft chalky ground is so good for growing things that people dig it up and send it to other states to be put on the ground to make vegetables grow better.

Long, long years ago, before there were any people in the world, the whole country was at the bottom of the sea, and much of the country was made under the sea just as Florida was made, from bones and shells of sea animals. This kind of bone and shell rock—for it is rock—is called *limestone*, because if you burn it it makes lime. Limestone is really bone-stone; stone made of the bones of sea animals. Then the earth wrinkled and crinkled and rose out of the water and formed the land. We know it was once under the sea because in many places now, high above the sea, even on mountain tops, we find this limestone with shells and bones of fish and other sea animals still showing in it. Marble, the most beautiful of all stone, is a kind of limestone, for it also is made of bone. People build houses and palaces of it and make statues and tombstones of marble or limestone.

Many of the people who go to Florida stop on their trip to see sights, and one of the greatest sights is in Virginia and Kentucky where the rock under the ground is all limestone. The "sights" are huge caves, and in Kentucky they are so large they are called Mammoth Caves. These caves have not been dug out by men but by water. Water, you know, melts

left: Picking tree-ripened oranges from a tree in one of the many citrus groves of Florida

sugar; but perhaps you didn't know that water melts rock too—not ordinary rock, but it melts limestone, and these caves are in limestone rock. The Mammoth Cave is like a huge cellar underground—a cave so large and high that you could put a whole city with its tall buildings in it. You could easily get lost and wander for miles. Men have been lost and unable to find their way out again and died and their skeletons have been found long years after.

Through the roof of the cave water drips drop by drop, and each drop leaves a bit of limestone, until in the course of time the dripping water makes icicles of rock that *hang down* from the roof of the cave. These are called *stalactites*. Drops of water from each icicle fall on to the floor of the cave, and the limestone gradually piles up and up like a stone post. These are called *stalagmites*. The trickling water also forms pools in the bottom of the cave, and in these pools of water live fish that are different from the fish in the water above ground. As it is pitch dark in the caves, these fish have no use for eyes, so after long, long years of living in the dark they have become blind.

---

right: Stalactites and stalagmites in Mammoth Cave, Kentucky

National Park Concessions, Inc. Photo by W. Ray Scott

Westward to
the Promised Land

Not so many years ago the Mississippi River was the far edge of the United States. Beyond the Mississippi it was wild—wilderness. Few people had ever been all the way across the country to the Pacific Ocean. There were Indians, wild animals, and high, high mountains in the way. Why did people want to go across the country anyway, and what sort of people were they? They were hunters who wanted to hunt wild animals, they were missionaries who wanted to make the Indians Christians, and they were people who were just inquisitive and who wanted to see what the wilderness was like.

Then one day a man told another, that another man had told him, that another man had told him, that still another man had told him that he had found gold in California, a land way off on the edge of the Pacific Ocean—plenty of gold; all you had to do was to dip it up in pans out of the rivers and pick it out of the sand and water.

Gold! Gold! It was almost as if someone had cried Fire! Thousands of people dropped their tools, stopped their farming, shut up their shops, loaded their beds and cooking things on wagons, put a cover over the wagon so that they could live under it, took along a gun, and rushed for the Far West to hunt for gold. There were no roads, there were no bridges, there were no signs to tell which was the right way—it was just wilderness. For months and months they traveled. Many of them were killed by Indians, many were drowned while crossing rivers, many lost their way and died of starvation or of thirst—but many also, at last, reached California, found gold just where they heard it was to be found, and made their fortunes. This was in the year 1849, so these people who went West were called "Forty-niners." Many of these people stayed to farm and settle on the land.

Since that time roads and railroads have been built all the way across the country and great cities have been built where once there was only wilderness.

The first railroad to the Pacific coast took the middle route from Chicago to San Francisco. But you can now take a train from Chicago and cross to the Pacific by the north, middle, or south. It took months when the Forty-niners went across in their covered wagons, but now it takes only a few hours by airplane.

People used to say, "Go West, young man, if you want to make a fortune," and many thousands did go West, not looking for gold, but for farmlands, which were given to them free by the United States if they would raise crops. Some of these men who went to Oklahoma and Texas and other places, chiefly west of the Mississippi, found oil in the ground on their farms. This oil spoiled the land for farming and made the water unfit even for the horses and cows to drink. The land was ruined—no good—so many farmers gave up and moved away.

There are three kinds of oil in the world—vegetable, animal, and mineral.

The oil from vegetables, like olive oil, and the oil from animals, like cod-liver oil, is good for food, but mineral oil from the rocks under the ground is not good for food. But someone found out that mineral oil could be burned to give light and heat, and then the automobile was invented, and from this mineral oil was made the gasoline to run automobiles. Many other things are now made from this kind of oil—medicine, colors for dying, and even perfumes and fabrics.

People who thought their farms had been spoiled by oil found that the oil was worth a fortune, worth much more than what they could make from chickens and pigs, or corn and wheat. Some wells had to be dug and the oil pumped up, but from others the oil sprouted up like a fountain—these were called gushers.

This oil that comes out of the rock underneath the ground is called *petroleum*, which means *rock oil*.

If you take a train by the middle route you cross Iowa, the corn state, passing through endless fields of corn. You next cross Nebraska. A city in Nebraska called Omaha is very important to anyone who likes to eat meat. There are many kinds of animals in the world, and yet of all these animals there are only three kinds that people generally eat. These three are the cow, the sheep, the pig. It takes millions of these animals every year to feed all the people in the United States, and millions of these animals are raised

Hollis Associates

Derricks over oil wells from which petroleum is pumped

91

in the states nearby and far from Omaha. These animals have to be fed, and the food that is best to make them fat is corn, so whole states grow corn, just to feed cows and sheep and pigs. The state of Iowa grows more corn than any other state. Some of the corn is shipped to Omaha, but most of it is shipped "on the hoof"—that is, it is fed to the animals and the animals are sent alive to Omaha to be killed. They are kept in big pens called stockyards until they are butchered. From Omaha they are sent in refrigerator cars or ships, everywhere, even to Europe. Omaha is the greatest butcher shop in the world.

above left: Close-up view of corn

---

middle left: Corn picker at work

---

below: Herd of cattle being driven across the plains

Aerial view of the cattle
pens at the stockyards in
Omaha, Nebraska

Gradually your train climbs higher and higher as the ground slopes gently upward, until you reach the state called Colorado. Colorado means "color red." Colorado is at the foot of the Rocky Mountains. The capital of the state is Denver, which is just about half-way from Chicago to the Pacific Ocean.

Not so far from Denver you can climb to the top of a Rocky Mountain peak, if you want to and if you have a good heart. The first man who tried to climb this mountain was named Pike, so ever since it has been called Pike's Peak. Pike couldn't climb to the top of his mountain, but nowadays thousands of people climb to the top each year just to see in how many hours they can do it. Pike's Peak is so high that there is often snow on the top in the summer as well as in the winter, and it is so high up that there is very little air to breathe when you are at the top. A great many people cannot stand it at the top; they have to sit down. They gasp for breath as if they had been running, or like a fish out of water; their hearts beat fast and hard and they feel faint and weak. There are now both a road and a railway up to the top, so that you don't have to climb Pike's Peak if you don't want to. The railway track, however, is so steep that an ordinary railway car would slide down like a sled, so the track has small iron steps between the rails, and the car has a wheel that catches into the steps so that it cannot slip backward or run away downhill. This kind of wheel is called a *cog*, and this kind of railway is called a cog railway.

top: Cog railway at Pike's Peak

left: Aerial view of Denver, Colorado, with the Rocky Mountains in the background

Wonders of the Land — the Grand Canyon, the Great Salt Lake, Yellowstone Park

One of the wonders in the West is a river. It is called the Colorado River, but it is not in the state of Colorado. It is in Arizona.

The river runs deep down in the bottom of the deepest "ditch" in the world, a gorge a mile deep in places. This gorge is called the Grand Canyon. You can stand on the edge of the canyon and look almost a mile down to what seems a slender little thread of water—the Colorado River—running at the bottom, and yet this little stream has cut this ditch in which it runs—worn it down—all by itself. Here we can see what the world looks like on the inside if we could dig down into it a mile deep, for here a little river has dug down a mile deep for us.

right: A view of the crevices and towering peaks of the Grand Canyon.

You can look across to the other side of the canyon and see the opposite wall almost a mile high—not a plain, blank wall like the wall of a building, but layers of rock, pile upon pile, colored yellow, red, green, orange, purple, mixed with sunshine and shadow. All of this rock was once under the sea, for it is limestone and sandstone. Each layer has been dyed a different color by minerals like iron and copper. If there was iron in the water, it turned the rock the color of iron rust—red; if copper, it turned the rock green.

Some of the branches of the Colorado run in smaller canyons, and high up on the walls of these canyons are houses built in caves in the rock. Once upon a time, long, long ago, people whom we call *cliff dwellers* built these homes there to be safe from their enemies.

A giant hop and skip north from the Grand Canyon would bring one to the state of Utah, where there is a great lake, but this great lake is different from the five "Great Lakes." The water in the five Great Lakes is fresh, the water in this great lake is salt, so it is called *Great Salt Lake*. As in the case of the ocean, rivers run into the Great Salt Lake, but no rivers run out of it.

What makes it salt?

The same thing that makes the ocean salt.

What makes the ocean salt?

The ground through which rivers flow has salts in it. Rivers, as they flow along, wash some of this salt out of the ground, carry it along, and dump it into the ocean. They carry so little salt at a time you would never know by tasting the river water that it was salt at all, but the rivers pour in this little bit of salt all the time, constantly, and so the salt gradually does collect in the ocean and in Great Salt Lake, for there is no way for the salt to go out once it's in the ocean or the lake. The water gets out of the lake as it does out of the ocean—by rising into the air as vapor—*evaporating*, we call it—but the salt doesn't evaporate, it can't rise into the air, and so it has no way of getting out.

opposite, top: A 440-foot suspension bridge on the Colorado River

opposite, bottom: Indian cliff dwellings, Mesa Verde

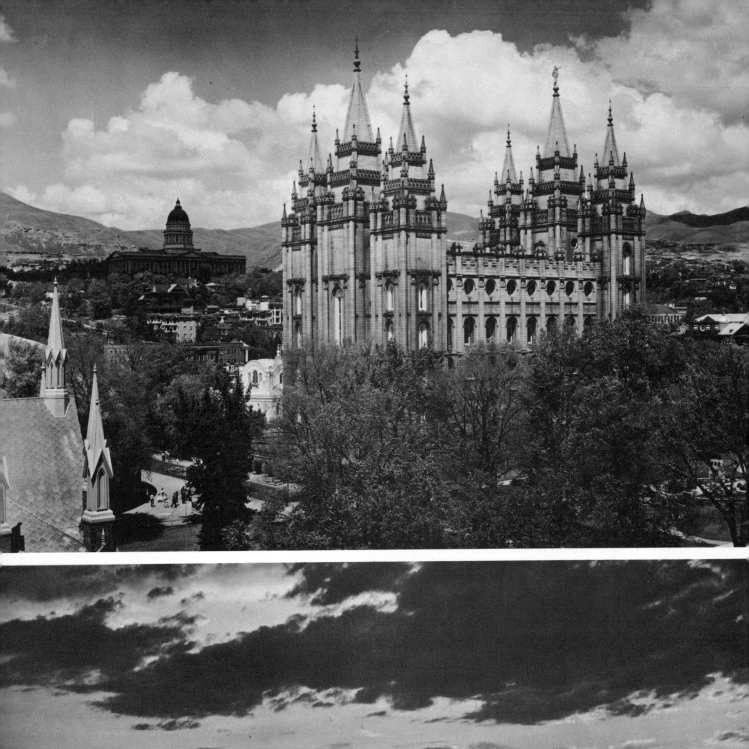

The Great Salt Lake is getting saltier and saltier all the time. It is already much saltier than the ocean. Salt water holds up a person or anything in it much better than fresh water, and the saltier the water the more it holds the person up. So in Great Salt Lake you couldn't drown whether you knew how to swim or not. You can stand in the water or sit in the water or lie down on the water as you would on a sofa. You can read the paper or eat your luncheon while sitting in the water, but you have to be very careful not to get any of the water in your eyes or in any small cut you may have on your body, for the salt water is so strong it smarts. Someday the ocean will be as salty as Great Salt Lake, for the ocean too is slowly, very slowly, getting saltier and saltier all the time. Then, even if there were a shipwreck, people would not drown—they would bob about in the sea like corks.

Still farther north, a hop, skip, and a jump from the Grand Canyon, in the corner of the state of Wyoming, is a place that looks on the map like a little state within the state. It is called Yellowstone Park. There are so many wonderful things in this part of the state that the United States thought people would like to see them, so they made a park of this corner of the state, with good roads and hotels, for people who wish to see the sights. No hunting is allowed, so wild animals and birds can live and raise families without being killed. There are bears in Yellowstone Park, but because they are not allowed to be hunted or shot, they become used to people and are not afraid of

opposite, top: The huge granite Mormon Temple in Salt Lake City, Utah. Salt Lake City, the capital of Utah, was settled in 1847 by Mormon pioneers under the leadership of Brigham Young.

opposite, bottom: Sundown at the Salt Lake Boat Harbor on the Great Salt Lake

right: An American Black Bear in Yellowstone Park, northwestern Wyoming.

them. But, it is wise for people to stay away from even these bears, for they are just as powerful and dangerous as bears anywhere.

The world in that part of the country has not yet cooled off altogether, and it is still very hot not far down under the ground. There are hundreds of springs in Yellowstone Park heated so hot by underground fires that they boil up and over like a pot on the fire.

There is a big lake in Yellowstone Park called Yellowstone Lake. You can stand on its edge and catch a fish in the lake and, without taking the fish off the hook, drop it into one of the hot springs near shore and cook it. In other places the water is blown up by the stream underneath into fountains. These fountains are called *geysers*, and some are quite big and some are quite beautiful. One called *Old Faithful* spouts regularly about once every hour, throwing a beautiful stream of water straight up into the air like a gigantic fire hose.

opposite: The Lone Star Geyser, one of the most spectacular geysers in Yellowstone National Park

below: Black bears in Yellowstone National Park

California—the Golden State

California was named after an island in an old fairy tale and in many ways the real California is a fairy-tale land. When gold was found in the rivers there, the story sounded like a fairy tale, but it turned out to be a true tale. Many stories they tell nowadays about California still sound like fairy tales to people in the East. Who would believe that there are trees in California so tall they seem to brush the sky—trees so big around that men have cut tunnels in them for automobiles to go through—trees so old that they were growing before Christ was born! It's true, there are. They are called Giant Redwoods. How wonderful it would be if those trees could tell us the true story of what has happened in their long lives!

California is the longest state in the United States. If you could take up California and put it down on the Atlantic coast it would stretch from Florida to New York.

California has one of the highest mountains in the United States. It is called Mount Whitney. Only Mt. McKinley in Alaska is higher.

California has the lowest place in America. It's a valley, and the valley is more than two hundred feet lower than the ocean. It is so dry and so hot down in this lowest hollow that nothing can live there except horned toads and lizards. They both love heat—the more heat the better for them. This low, hot valley is called Death Valley. People usually keep away from it, but some men have strayed into it looking for gold and have lost their way, or some who wanted to get to the other side tried to cross it and before they could get out or reach the other side they died of heat or thirst. That's why it is called Death Valley.

Besides Death Valley, California has many other valleys. One of the loveliest of these valleys is called the *Yosemite*. It is a very deep trough, and streams of water fall over the edge into the trough from many high places. One of these falls turns to mist before it reaches the ground and looks

Gabriel Moulin, SF

above left: Redwood trees in Redwood State Park, California

above right: Yosemite Falls, Yosemite National Park

like a huge veil, so it is called the Bridal Veil Falls. Half a dozen of these waterfalls in the Yosemite Valley are higher than Niagara, and two of them tumble head-long a quarter of a mile from the top to the bottom of the valley—the highest falls in America.

California has oranges, lemons, and grapefruit, too, but they didn't *come* from California; they *went* there. There were no oranges and no lemons growing in America at all before explorers came to this country. The first settlers in California came from the country of Spain on the other side of the Atlantic Ocean. In Spain oranges and lemons grew, and the Spaniards brought over orange and lemon plants and started them growing in California and also in Florida.

The Spaniards built houses like those in Spain, with white stucco walls and red tile roofs and with yards called *patios* in the center of the house. They gave their cities Spanish names like Los Angeles, which means The Angels; they named many of their cities after saints—San Francisco after St. Francis, Santa Barbara after St. Barbara—for many of the Spaniards were priests, who built mission churches up and down the land.

The City of the Angels is now the largest city on the Pacific coast. Near Los Angeles is Hollywood, where the weather is fine most of the time for taking moving pictures. This is one reason why it is such a good place for making movies, but another is that there are so many different kinds of natural scenery nearby. If they want to make a picture of a ship scene or shipwreck, there is the ocean. If they want to make a picture of the desert with camels and Arabs, there is the desert. If they want to make a picture in the hot countries, there are palms and flowers. If they want to make pictures of winter scenes, all they have to do is to go to the mountains nearby and there is snow and ice all the year round.

The city of San Francisco on the coast north of Los Angeles is nearly as large as Los Angeles. It might have been larger, but not so many years ago a terrible earthquake shook down the city. The quake only lasted a few minutes, but in that few minutes it rocked the city, cracked open the ground, and knocked down buildings as if they were houses of children's blocks, and hundreds and hundreds of people were killed. But the worst thing the

109

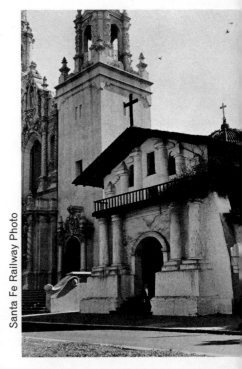

above: Mission Dolores, one of the original California adobe missions

opposite, top: City Hall, San Francisco

opposite, bottom: Nighttime finds the fishing fleet anchored in the harbor at Fisherman's Wharf, San Francisco

American Airlines

earthquake did was to upset stoves and lamps that started one of the worst fires ever known—a fire that burned up most of the city. Were the people discouraged? Not at all. They collected their insurance money—and they built the city up again.

San Francisco has one of the finest harbors in the world. Its harbor is a long bay—fifty miles long. Ships enter the harbor from the Pacific Ocean through an opening called the Golden Gate. The city is built on many hills so steep that it is difficult for automobiles to climb them, but houses built on them have lovely views of the ocean, the bay, or the Golden Gate. Across the Golden Gate is a huge suspension bridge almost as big as the Verrazzano-Narrows Bridge in New York City.

Ships enter and leave San Francisco for all the countries in the world. Across the Pacific Ocean are China and Japan, and in days gone by so many Chinese came to the United States and landed in San Francisco that there is a part of the city called Chinatown, where there are Chinese houses and shops and theaters. This is the largest Chinese settlement outside the Orient. Many Japanese too came to the United States from Japan, and bought farms where they raised fruits and vegetables.

left: Moonlight fishing near Golden Gate Bridge, San Francisco

Alaska and the
Pacific Northwest

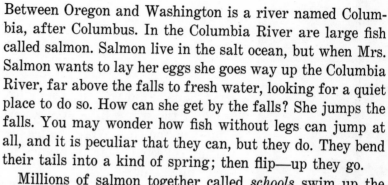

Between Oregon and Washington is a river named Columbia, after Columbus. In the Columbia River are large fish called salmon. Salmon live in the salt ocean, but when Mrs. Salmon wants to lay her eggs she goes way up the Columbia River, far above the falls to fresh water, looking for a quiet place to do so. How can she get by the falls? She jumps the falls. You may wonder how fish without legs can jump at all, and it is peculiar that they can, but they do. They bend their tails into a kind of spring; then flip—up they go.

Millions of salmon together called *schools* swim up the river. Fishermen catch them in nets, but they leave most of them so that they can lay eggs from which little salmon are born. The little salmon swim down the river and out into the ocean, where they live and grow up until it comes time for them also to lay eggs, and then they in their turn swim up the river, jump up the falls, and are either caught or left to raise more families of little salmon. Salmon meat is pink; we call it salmon color. It is packed in cans. You may have eaten salmon from the Columbia River.

Delicious apples grow in the state of Washington. People in Washington, D.C.—all the way across the country—buy apples that have been shipped from Washington state— 3,000 miles away—for they are so much better than ordinary apples. They are *skookum*. That's what the Indians of the Northwest call something very nice.

There are great forests in Washington and Oregon. The forest trees are cut down to make lumber for building houses and paper to write on.

At the northwest corner of America is a large country that is part of the United States. It is the state of Alaska. The highest mountain in the United States is there. It is called Mount McKinley. Alaska is so cold, so far off, and so hard to get to, and yet before Alaska became a state the United States bought it and paid millions of dollars for it, not because it had the highest mountain, but mainly because of the fish in its waters and the fur on its animals. And then one day gold was discovered there.

above: Jumping salmon

top left: Majestic Mt. Hood dominates this scene of Timothy Lake and the fir-forested slopes of Oregon's mountains

bottom left: The fish ladders at Bonneville Dam, Oregon, allow salmon to go around the dam and swim upriver to spawning grounds on the upper Columbia tributaries

The Sun and Raven Totem,
near Ketchikan, Alaska,
tells the story of a
great flood and how
Raven helped man to survive.
The Alaskan Indian is
considered the best of the
totemic carvers.

Gold is a magic word. Again, as in the days of the Forty-niners, thousands of people, when they heard of the gold, left everything and, with nothing but shovels to dig the gold and sieves to strain it out of the water, started off to that faraway place, hoping to make their fortunes before the new year. Many foolishly went off with nothing to live on after they reached Alaska. They didn't seem to know that where the gold was to be found there was no food, nothing to eat, and no stores where one could buy food. Others, who were wiser, carried cans of food with them, and when the foolish gold diggers had found gold, the wise ones sold them food for their gold. For a can of beans they often asked hundreds of times what it had cost, and the foolish gold diggers had to pay it or starve, for they couldn't eat gold and they had to eat or they would die. So the wise ones came back with the gold which the foolish ones had dug, and the foolish ones were lucky to get back at all.

In the parts of Alaska where fish can be caught for food, Indians live in small villages. In the center of each village they put up a tall pole carved and painted in the forms of birds and animals with big ugly faces. These are called totem poles. Each tribe or family has some bird or animal such as an eagle or a bear for its mascot, and the totem pole is the tribe's sign.

In Alaska at night the whole northern sky is often hung suddenly with curtains of fire and becomes ablaze with flashing flames shooting from the ground far up into the heavens. It looks as if the world were on fire and were about to explode. This amazing sight is called the *Aurora Borealis* or *Northern Lights*. It may be seen often in Alaska and sometimes, though perhaps only once or twice in a lifetime, much farther south. It is a terrifying sight to those who have never seen or even heard of such a thing before, and yet the Aurora Borealis does no more harm than a beautiful sunset or a rainbow in the sky.

What causes the Aurora Borealis? That's a hard question to answer. Electricity has something to do with it and so have sun spots. Have you ever heard of sun spots? Sometimes a dark spot will appear on the sun and move slowly across it. You can't see sun spots because the sun is much too bright to be stared at. But men who look through telescopes with darkened glass to protect their eyes can see these spots and they can photograph them with special cameras. After a sun spot appears on the sun there is usually a very bright Aurora Borealis.

above: The Northern Lights blazing in Alaskan skies

top left: An Alaskan Eskimo peers from his sod igloo home.

bottom left: An Eskimo boy at King Island Village near Nome, Alaska

The Hawaiian Islands

Near the middle of the Pacific Ocean are the Hawaiian Islands. These islands were formed when a huge crack opened up on the ocean floor. Lava came up through the crack for millions and millions of years and formed a series of very high mountains. The tops of these mountains eventually rose above the ocean to form the islands that in 1959 became the newest state in the Union.

Honolulu is the capital of the state, and its harbor is called "The Crossroads of the Pacific" because so many ships stop there on the way to and from other places.

In Hawaii are raised most of the pineapples we eat, and there are many sugar cane plantations.

The other Hawaiian Islands are very beautiful, with mountains, forests, valleys, rivers, beaches, bays, and farmlands. Beautiful, brilliantly colored flowers grow all year round in the mild climate—orchids, roses, hibiscus, gardenias, and many, many others.

Hawaii is a wonderful place to visit, for the people who live there are among the friendliest anywhere. A mixture of people of different races live on the islands together, work together, and get along so well with each other that it seems strange that all people everywhere can't seem to do the same thing.

opposite, top: The Waimea Canyon on the island of Kauai, Hawaii, is often called the Grand Canyon of the Pacific

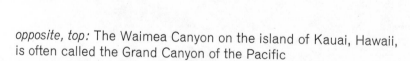

opposite, bottom: Passenger liners tie up alongside Aloha Tower in Honolulu Harbor. Honolulu is one of the most beautiful cities in the world, with a green mountain backdrop and circled by blue seas.

Polynesians were the first people who lived in Hawaii that we know anything about. They came by canoe during the years from about 700 to 1100 A.D. The Polynesians fished and grew many different kinds of foods. Some of the foods they grew came from plants and seeds that they had brought with them from Asia. These things still grow on the islands today.

Captain James Cook, an Englishman, discovered the islands in 1778, and after that, many foreigners came to live there. In the early 1800's many New England missionaries came to the islands. During and after the middle 1800's people were brought from China and Japan to work on the sugar plantations. Then, in the early 1900's, Portuguese, Spaniards, and Filipinos went to Hawaii to work on the plantations. Since that time many other groups of immigrants have settled in Hawaii, and now they all work in various jobs on the islands.

There is an excellent university in Honolulu, where more than 6,000 students go to classes every year. Many students from the mainland of the United States are attracted to this university because of the beauty of the islands, the beautiful weather, the opportunities for water sports such as swimming, boating, and surfboarding, and the friendliness of the people.

When a visitor comes to Honolulu the Hawaiians throw a garland of flowers called a lei over his head, and when the visitor leaves he throws the lei into the water. This custom is to insure his return some day. There is one word the Hawaiians use very often; it is *Aloha*. Aloha means "hello, welcome, good-by, God bless you." The spirit of the islands can be summed up in this word which gives the feeling of love, hospitality, and friendliness.

Aloha!

left: Near the city of Lahaina on the Island of Maui, Hawaii

right: Kaanapali Beach, Maui, Hawaii

Puerto Rico

Puerto Rico is an island in the Caribbean Sea. It belongs to the United States but in a very unusual way. Puerto Rico is a commonwealth, and that means that it is more independent than the states. It is almost like a country.

All Puerto Ricans are citizens of the United States. They don't need passports to go to any of the states. People from the states don't need passports to go to Puerto Rico either. But Puerto Ricans do not pay any taxes to the United States government. They pay taxes only to the Commonwealth of Puerto Rico. Of course, since Puerto Ricans do not pay taxes to the United States government, the government does not do some of the things for them that it does for the people of the states. Puerto Ricans have to do many more things for themselves.

As a commonwealth of the United States, Puerto Rico has free trade with the United States. That means that things made in Puerto Rico can be sold anywhere in the United States without having special taxes, called import duty, added to them by the United States government. This is very important to the Puerto Rican people, because the United States is their best customer. If all of the things that Puerto Rico sold to people in the states had import duty added to their cost, they would be very expensive. The people in the United States could not buy as many of them. Sugar cane is one of the most important things that Puerto Rico sends to the United States.

Puerto Rico is important to the defense of all of the lands of the United States. Puerto Ricans serve in the military, because they are United States citizens. Puerto Ricans let the United States have military bases on the island also. You see, Puerto Rico does not act for itself when it comes to dealing with the rest of the world. It acts as a part of the United States. Sometimes the President of the United States asks important Puerto Ricans to be special representatives of the United States. Puerto Ricans have been especially good representatives to some of the South American countries.

opposite, top: Sugar cane being loaded for transportation to the sugar mills, Puerto Rico

opposite, bottom: Tobacco fields, Puerto Rico

Why would Puerto Ricans do so well with South Americans? Well, the traditions and background of the Puerto Rican people are like the traditions and background of the South Americans. Puerto Ricans have a Spanish background. Even though most Puerto Ricans speak some English, their native tongue is Spanish. They look at a lot of things the way Spanish-speaking people do. That is because of their history.

The island of Puerto Rico seems to have been very popular with explorers and conquerors. Columbus went there on his second voyage. That was in 1493. Poncé de Leon was with him at the time, and he remembered the island later and went back. He sailed his ship into a natural harbor of the island and named that harbor "Puerto Rico." The words "Puerto Rico" are Spanish for "rich port." He named the island "San Juan Bautista." In English that means "St. John the Baptist."

Later, the island was called Puerto Rico and the capital was called San Juan. One of the important cities in Puerto Rico is called Poncé, after Poncé de Leon.

The French, the English, and the Dutch all tried to capture Puerto Rico from the Spanish. To defend the island, the Spanish built a fortress called El Morro, which means "the bluff." They called it that because the fortress stands on a bluff that overlooks San Juan Harbor. The fortress is still standing, even though building on it began as long ago as 1539. It is a favorite sight-seeing place for tourists.

When the United States won the Spanish-American War in 1898, it took Puerto Rico for its own. The United States ruled the island and the people. In 1917, the people became United States citizens, but they were still ruled by a governor from the United States. Finally, in 1948, they were given a right to elect their own governor. Then in 1952, they became an independent commonwealth that rules itself. Puerto Rico elects a commissioner to the United States Congress. This commissioner has no vote in the Congress, however.

Puerto Rico makes its money from its industries. Tourism is the biggest industry. Most of the tourists come from the states. They like to visit the island because it is beautiful. Even though the sun shines most of the time, the island does not get too hot, because the trade winds always make a nice breeze. Puerto Rico has beautiful beaches and hotels and other things that tourists like, too.

Air France Photo

The 200-year-old
Church of San German
in the ancient town of
San German, Puerto Rico

above: San Juan Gate, the main entrance to the walled city of San Juan and the only remaining gate in the walls of the old city

top left: View of the lower ramparts of El Morro as seen through an archway of the main fort

bottom left: Luxurious hotels in San Juan

INDEX: *Young People's Story of the Americas: The United States and its Possessions*

Type   *Century Expanded*
Typesetter   *American Typesetting Corporation*
Printer   *The Regensteiner Corporation*